YOU
are Not
HERE
by
ACCIDENT

You are Divinely placed with a powerful purpose!

CHARLANA KELLY

You are Not Here by Accident
You are Divinely placed with a powerful purpose!
© 2017 by Charlana Kelly
All Rights Reserved

Creative Director, Cover Design & Layout: Leslie Kinney

SPEAK
TRUTH
Media Group LLC

a SpeakTruth Media Book

ISBN (Print): 978-0-9985190-0-5
ISBN (eBook): 978-0-9985190-1-2

DEDICATION

To everyone who believes they have a greater purpose
than what they are living today.

All glory to God

forever and ever, amen!

much love to my sweet friend Brenda Charlene

Contents

Chapters

Praise for… You are Not Here by Accident

This amazing work "You are Not Here by Accident" authored by the powerful and eloquent Charlana Kelly is alive and rich with God's love, filled with His wisdom and great truth. Her words will inspire readers to see and accept themselves as more; called to more and here right now for more than they can imagine today! Charlana's knowledge of the Word of God coupled with her gift of loving encouragement will cheer readers on to discover their own greatness in Christ. I look forward to seeing the mountains that will be moved in the near future as a result of the message this book contains. Thank you Charlana.

—Tracey Schreiber, Designer & "Ideator" at The Fairytale Studio Houston TX

I found, "You Are Not Here by Accident," to be a powerful manifesto for everyone who calls themselves a believer. Charlana has written a clear, relatable, and concise encouragement for us all to rediscover a gospel surrendered life; a life worth pursuing, released from the heart of God and uniquely fashioned for each one of us.

—James Wheeler, Worship Pastor at The Church of Grace and Peace Tom's River NJ

I was encouraged as I read Charlana's book, "You are Not Here by Accident." How refreshing to be inspired and empowered in my Christian walk, confirmed that I am fashioned in God's plan for my life and not reminded again and again of a postmodern worldview that focuses more on self than Savior. This work brilliantly exposes our need to affirm our individual significance in Christ. Needful, especially since, we live in an age that leaves us frustrated, defeated, and powerless by a culture determined to shape our worth only through comparison to others. Yes, people are highly valued but only through exposing their value and worth in light of the Creator, and His love and purpose for His children. It reminds me of William Blake's words, "This life's dim windows of the soul distorts the heavens from pole to pole and leads you to believe a lie when you see with, not through, the eye." This generation often sees life with their own eyes, when they were created to see the world through their conscience. In the end, it is only God's truth that gives us value, after all He created us to be a true reflection of Himself.

—Tim Allen, M. Phil. Senior Pastor at First Christian Church Crockett TX

"You are Not Here by Accident" is one of the best books I have read concerning purpose! Great for new converts, as well as those who are ready to get right in middle of their role as ambassadors for Christ. I cannot imagine a better book on discipleship!

—Larry Bruce, Pastor at The Fellowship at Larry Bruce Gardens Kennard TX

"You are Not Here by Accident" is packed full of answers to questions we all have at some point in our life about who we are and why we exist. As I read this book I could hear the passion of Charlana's heart for all to know Christ and live the life God created us for. I was so moved that tears filled my eyes as I thought about the opportunity people will have to finally get free of the lies the world has offered us about our identity. Truth comes pouring through the words in this book, truth that brings freedom, freedom that allows God to reveal His love and purpose for our lives and then empower us to walk it out. I was truly inspired, challenged and strengthened and I pray all who read it will be also.

—Barbara Michael, Pastor & Teacher at Barbara Michael Ministries in Inverness FL

This book is amazing! "You are Not Here by Accident" is full of faith, encouragement and wisdom! It is the exact message that I dearly wish every child was taught from birth because that would give them all a head start into this amazing life of Christ before each of us! So well written by Charlana Kelly and easy to understand; this book is for people who are new to faith as well as those of us who just need a reminder of these great truths. Thank you Charlana for writing this amazing tool that I can now give to all my friends and family to bless them and encourage them in this incredible adventure of faith!

—Beverly Carter, Houston Texas

"You are Not Here by Accident" is a guide that will assist you in practical ways on your walk from who you think you are, to who you actually are, which is who God says you are! You will experience the transition from alone to loved, from wandering to a life with purpose and a path. As you read, allow yourself to be opened to the things that the Holy Spirit wants to do in your life.

—Travis Stewart, Founder & President of The Jesus Way Inc., Kingston Jamaica

Like a properly brewed Sweet Tea on a hot summer day, Charlana Kelly's book is a refreshing drink that encourages the soul. Powerfully hopeful, you will find yourself going back to highlighted chapters in the wee hours of the evening to hear her kind words direct from God's heart. In "You are Not Here by Accident," Charlana chronicles a process to get moving in the purposes of God with the same Southern grace she carries in person. An authentic and beautiful read

—Ann McDonald, Orinda CA

As a Healing & Deliverance Minister, one of the greatest challenges we see in ministry is identity issues. The root of this is believing the lie that you are not wanted or have no purpose in life. "You are Not Here by Accident" exemplifies the truth about who God created you to be and why God created you. Charlana uses her gift of grace, coupled with knowledge and understanding, to encourage and affirm readers to purpose. Very motivating!

—Karin Hockman, Founder of Wings Worldwide, Reno NV

Ah, the age old question, "Why am I here?" Find out how to find out as you read "You are Not Here by Accident." Know that God has ordained your steps and can even make use of your missteps.

—Tim Devolve, Founder & President of The Patriotic Remnant, Los Angeles CA

Introduction

YOU, yes you—you are not here by accident!

Do those words evoke a response in your heart? Are you excited about the fact that your existence is not an accident? Are you afraid of what I might say to you in this book? Or, do you already know there is more for you this side of heaven than you are experiencing today? I can tell you emphatically that the Lord put this book on my heart with YOU in mind.

My greatest joy doesn't come from my own achievements but from witnessing the achievements of others who dare to believe God. Those who trusted Him in days gone by walked in great places. Albeit they went with hearts pounding and knees shaking, but they had the courage to step over their fear and step out of the boat into deep waters with Jesus. YOU my friend were created to do the same! Let's take that step together for Him!

You are the reason I'm praying and thinking, and why I was inspired to write this book. I want you to get it! I want you to be ALL God created you to be! I want you to do EVERYTHING God has created to you do. I want you to be a nation-changer, a soil-shaker (thanks Joshua Botello), and, a soul-reaper. You are, you can, and I pray you will with the power of God working in and through you for His glory.

I find often though that some people lack the inspiration, confidence, courage and boldness to do what they know in their heart God is asking them to do. I pray the message in this book will change your heart, mind, desire, and determination to follow Him out into unfamiliar territory where the true riches of Christ can be found.

And, I realize that a book is not often the ultimate catalyst for moving the masses, if it were the lion would have already laid down with the lamb. Reading this book is just the first step. Afterwards, it's time to consider the high call on your life. The unique personal assignment God has created you to complete.

You are part of a fierce army of ordinary people called to do extraordinary things. There is more in you than you can imagine today. The message in this book will help you realize your purpose and accept your Divine position as a key-player in the most amazing move God has done among His people since the beginning of time.

I want to help you find that assignment and develop a strategy for implementation. I want to see you SOAR with the eagles exactly the way Isaiah 40[1] says you will.

I want to teach and train you to be mighty in God's kingdom, to pursue every Divine opportunity and Kairos moment, and to position yourself for maximum impact as the Kingdom of God continues to increase throughout the earth in this hour.

More than likely you are going to have to change the way you think and what you believe about yourself, replacing both with what God believes and says about you. This is not a five-minute process, it's a daily pursuit that all believers must commit to.

I know people who have written daily confessions and Scriptures on Post-it® Notes and stuck them all over their home. Well, actually... I have done it too! Constant reminders of the truth about what God has to say about you will help in the process of renewing your mind and your heart, while transforming your future as a result. I encourage you to follow suit with your peers. I promise you, you will be grateful you did.

And, I've included an "Application & Activation" section at the end of each chapter to help you along the way.

Now... Are you ready? I hope you are! Either way...

Let's go!

1

God's Story of YOU

"You are the only you God made... God made you and broke the mold." – Max Lucado

Created in His Image

You were created in the image of God, uniquely fashioned for His Divine purpose. It is special to think that the Creator of the Universe had you on His mind, considered all of your days, and then blessed you the moment you chose Christ.

Your life in Christ begins at salvation, but what about before you chose Him. Was God not ever-present in your life and affairs? No! He has been with you from the beginning. Your Abba Father has been in hot pursuit of you. In fact, He chose you before you ever found Him[1].

At every turn from the moment you entered the world through your mother's womb, God positioned people and events in your life to draw you to Him. He had a plan, He numbered your days, and called you by name. He created you for relationship with Himself and for others as a testimony of His goodness to His people.

The unsaved are looking for you. In every arena of your life, there are people whose hearts are crying out for relief from burdens and pains. You have exactly what they need and God wants to provide for them through you. God works through people. He doesn't have to; He chooses to. So you are the expression of God that calls out to others saying, "Do you know Him?" You may not have ever said those words, but there's a presence upon you that draws them to Him.

God is Spirit, since we are created in His image we too are spirit. In fact, the Hebrew word for the expression "in His image" (tselem) is plural; likenesses, images, even phantom (This "phantom" is the Holy Spirit inside that cannot be seen with the natural eye!).

What does this reveal? There are three expressions of God; Father, Son, Holy Spirit. There are also three expressions of you; spirit, soul, body. God's creation is perfect and when He said let "US" make man in "OUR" image He was speaking plural. You are wholly divine in creation, as you grow in Him and become the complete expression of Jesus on earth. This is the calling of all of God's people.

Created to Relate

While we are the image of God, we were also created to relate; first to Him and second to others. We relate in life by fellowship and communication.

Fellowship is fulfilled as we gather together in His name; living, learning, and growing in Christ. Communication on the other hand is multi-faceted. It is spiritual, experiential, and observational.

Spiritual communication is spirit to spirit, by way of the Holy Spirit. This type of communication occurs most often through prayer. It is also a result of what I call "electric thoughts" that you know are not your own, but answers from the Lord regarding questions you've asked in prayer.

Experiential communication is our encounter with God through events. This type of communication occurs when you feel peace envelope you or a sense of love overwhelm you. Both examples of God's presence drawing near to you. Experiential communication can also happen when a miracle unfolds in a situation and you know God has intervened on your behalf.

Observational communication comes through nature or interaction when we witness something that displays or declares the glory and majesty of God. This type of communication produces a deeper understanding of God and His promises in the Word.

God wants to speak with you, this is how He relates to you. He does so through prayer and communion in His presence. He speaks through His Word, people, dreams, and nature. Expect Him to communicate and position yourself to hear Him when He does!

God has created you for communication too. It's time to speak, declare and proclaim the Lord throughout the land.

Don't rely on your pastor and Christian friends to do all the talking. You, my friend, are called to communicate. If that frightens you, then all the more I believe God has called you to be the voice of His kingdom on earth. It's easier than you think, just be willing to share your experiences and observations about your relationship with Jesus and your amazing Father God.

The Beautiful Love Story Unfolds

One of the most amazing parts of confirming Scripture about your life from beginning to end can be found in Psalm 139. Here's just a tiny taste from The Passion Translation[2]; "You saw who You created me to be, before I ever became me" verse 16.

I can't fathom that God's thoughts toward me began before I ever took my first breath. He planned out all of my days and wrote them in a book before I ever set foot on the earth. These are thoughts too wonderful for me to comprehend. Yet they are truth about the great passion God has for His people. The same passion He has for YOU.

His plans are good. His blessing already bestowed on you regardless of what your life circumstances have been to now. You are chosen for a blessing.

I feel compelled to diverge here for a moment and speak a word to those whose life has not yet seen the bounty of God's blessing.

You were *not* chosen for pain, nor established to be destroyed. If pain has come to you through the hands of others, it comes as a result of a person who is walking in darkness.

This was not the plan of God for you or the other party. His plan for all is that we would choose His ways, choose Christ, choose life and live. In doing so, we are delivered from darkness and brought into His kingdom of Christ where goodness and blessing flow[3].

Often people find themselves in broken situations, but it's never God's plan for them to be destroyed by it. He desires to repair our brokenness and restore us back to wholeness in Christ.

So if you are still in a broken place, know this, God has prepared a way of healing and restoration for you. Choose life, live and learn with Him and walk with Him to completion. Spirit first, through salvation in Christ; then soul and body, as you put to practice the wisdom He provides through His Word.

The best part of finding wholeness in Him is through a revelation of His unfailing love. It never runs out! When God pours His loving kindness on you the flow never ends. He never stops pouring, you are ever filled and overflowing; spilling out on everyone around you, touching them with that same unconditional love that first touched you.

This is the great love story that has unfolded to generations both past, present and future. You are the recipient of what the entire world longs to have, but gropes in darkness with no end. You are the epistle they long to find and read and realize. Your story is greater than you know today. You have to live it though. You have to be willing to take the hand of God, believe in Christ, allow His Lordship to take hold of you, then yield to the leading of the Holy Spirit. As you do, His plans for you will unfold, and every jot and tittle of the words written in the book about you will be fulfilled.

> "You are the recipient of what the entire world longs to have. You are the epistle they long to find and read and realize."

You are a Part of His Story

Isn't it interesting that "HIStory" appears to be a combination of two words? We have a personal history, but then there's the history of God's plan and family unfolding daily, that we are a part of bringing to pass. Remember you are living out a book already written. God spoke the end from the beginning, so your story is complete. Still, you have to live out your part for the entire story to be exactly what He desired.

Since God knew the end from the beginning, He knew the exact time you would be here. You are not a random selection! It is even Divine that you are here, right now, reading this book. He knew I would write this book and that you would read it. There is a purpose in it all. But no *chance* at all.

There are three English words that are not translatable in Hebrew; religion, fair, and coincidence. There are no coincidences with God, every person is put into place at the perfect time. All for His glory and praise.

This is where some people get into sticky territory about foreknowledge or predestation, which causes misunderstanding about the goodness of God. Calvinists (Those who follow the doctrinal beliefs of John Calvin[4], 1509—1564) believe God predetermined who would and would not receive salvation, which totally denies grace and free will.

The Scripture is replete with references to God's desire that all come to the knowledge of Truth (Jesus!) and that none would perish. Don't get twisted up with foreknowledge and predestation in your mind. Because God knew past, present and future, of course, He knew who would receive Christ and who would harden their heart. Nevertheless, He still gives everyone an opportunity to hear and receive. He is a good, good Father and that will NEVER change.

So, God's story of You was written many millenia ago with joy, peace, much love and great expectation for your arrival! Since you first beleived Holy Spirit has been teaching you along the pathway of God's purpose for your life, so—rejoice!

Application & Activation

Settle this ...

- You are created in the image of God.
- He knew you and numbered your days before you were in your mother's womb.
- You have a purpose to fulfill.

Scripture meditations ...

Psalm 139:13-16

"You made all the delicate, inner parts of my body and knit me together in my mother's womb. Thank you for making me so wonderfully complex! Your workmanship is marvelous—how well I know it. You watched me as I was being formed in utter seclusion, as I was woven together in the dark of the womb. You saw me before I was born. Every day of my life was recorded in your book. Every moment was laid out before a single day had passed."

Romans 8:29

"For God knew his people in advance, and he chose them to become like his Son, so that his Son would be the firstborn among many brothers and sisters."

Ephesians 1:4

"Even before he made the world, God loved us and chose us in Christ to be holy and without fault in his eyes."

Journal & Pray ...

Write out the purpose you believe you were created to fulfill. This is progressive, but you can identify it by your passion or reoccurring moments where you find yourself in a position to bring a common answer to a situation. Ask Holy Spirit to reveal your purpose and help you fulfill it. He will. Write it out.

2

Handpicked for Purpose

"You are not unwanted; you were chosen. You are not unloved; you were to die for. You are not alone; you are His!" – Unknown

"Handpicked" means to carefully select with a particular purpose in mind. Synonyms include; chosen, invited, elite, and choice[1]. Both Jesus and Paul spoke specifically about the fact that you have been chosen[2]. The Greek word is the same for both verses (eklegó) meaning to select (choose) out of, by a highly deliberate choice (i.e. real heart-preference) with a definite outcome (as with the destination of divine selection for salvation)[3].

If you have never felt special in your life, now would be a good time to realize just how special you are to God. It's hard to comprehend the greatness of God's impact, fingerprint, and purpose that is already written on your heart. But, part of growing in the Lord is accepting who you are not just *to* Him but *for* Him.

Ultimate Destination

You are an exact replication of Christ, albeit you are under construction, your ultimate destination is to be transformed into His image and likeness (2 Corinthians 3:18). Divine in every way; a child of God with full heavenly privilege, changing day-by-day with an ever-intensifying measure of His glory.

Uniquely Purposed

While all believers are being transformed, each person has a unique purpose that only he/she can fulfill. This purpose begins personally with everyday living, then extends outward to others. First, family, then church, then neighborhood, marketplace, institutions, etc.

"You are an exact replication of Christ, albeit you are under construction, your ultimate destination is to be transformed into the image and likeness of Christ."

We all have a field or garden so to speak. This is our realm of influence. Our influence is for people to persuade them through our daily living with the Good News of Jesus. God has divinely placed every single person in your pathway. You were chosen for your parents, your siblings, and extended family. You were chosen for your spouse, your children, and beyond. You were chosen for your neighbors, co-workers, city, and beyond. These are all examples of your field which expands as you garner more influence and prove your faithfulness to the Lord.

Faithful in Least, Ruler of Much

Everyone starts small. When you prove yourself faithful with little or few, God will make you ruler over much. You are being prepared to rule with Christ, so this process of proving faithfulness takes you closer and closer to the ultimate purpose you were created for.

God will never give you more than you can handle. He is watching though to see how you handle what He has entrusted to your care. He is particularly interested in how you will handle the people He brings into your life. People are of utmost importance to Him, because He doesn't desire that any would perish but that all would come to repentance, be saved and come to the knowledge of truth[4].

He's using you to show Christ to them either by demonstration or communication. Mostly by daily living! Daily doings often speak louder than daily sayings. People who watch believers are often watching to see when they mess up, but imagine a life with few failings and many victories while giving God glory through it all. Or imagine a life-storm where most would worry and scurry to fix it themselves, but those who know their God are standing firm in faith not wavering at God's promises[5].

When the "worried" witness the victory of the "faithful," they see how God defends and upholds His steadfast followers through every trial. As the righteous rejoice in their Father's mighty hand, the "worried" are drawn to Him through them.

Who are you drawn to? Who do you want in your corner when adversity hits? I want someone who will not commiserate with me, but call me up in faith and point me to the promise of God.

The people who point you to promise are the ones who are fulfilling what God has created them to do, they are like a "road sign" directing others upward to God in Christ! You too are a "road sign" to others along the pathway to Jesus.

The Gift

This purpose or unique calling and gift that God has given you for His glory, must be discovered. Most people never find it. So, they live their life by default, missing the best of God's plan. I want to encourage you to consider your gifts, ask God to help you use them for His glory, then step out boldly and do what He shows you to do.

I've heard it said that cemeteries are the saddest places on earth and surely they are. There are a lot of unfulfilled gifts and calls represented on the cemetery grounds. I have to agree! My heart gets heavy at the thought people live their entire life never uncovering their God given gifts and talents.

The last thing I want to do is stand before the Lord and see everything I missed; people, opportunities, experiences. How tragic is it that we were created to do something great for God, but only skimmed the surface of it? Or, missed it altogether. Please don't let that be YOU!

Your gifts are for His glory. Whether music, speaking, dancing, painting, building, athletic, creative, engineering, leading, business, all are given by God for display of His greatness in the earth.

Often talented people have no idea their gift even comes from God. It's not until you realize every good and perfect gift[6] comes from Him, that knowledge shifts to understanding the purpose of the gift.

There's no greater gift we could give to our Father, than to offer our talent back to Him for His service in the Kingdom of God. After all the special abilities we possess came from Him in the first place, we are giving it back to bring glory to Him. Think of this, God gave His best to us in Jesus, ought we to give Him our best by offering back to Him the talent He gave us to begin with.

Beholding the Mirror Image

The Scripture speaks of you with grandeur. Words like pillar, tree, son, daughter, royal, ambassador, gate. Adjectives like flourish, prosper, overcomer, conqueror all refer to God's chosen people.

One of the most beautiful descriptions of a purpose God has created you for comes from 2 Corinthians 3 where Paul calls you a "minister of the New Covenant." He said that you are a letter from Christ, with words written by the Spirit of the Living God inscribed forever on your heart. He refers to you as a living epistle being read and known by all. Some describe this as a love poem written by God to all of humanity through you.

You are also described as a "masterpiece[7];" a unique one-of-a-kind creation. No one else like you in all of the generations past, present and future.

> **"You will not become what God created you to be until you see yourself as He sees you."**

Here's the challenge in all of these matters. What you think about yourself overshadows God's thoughts about you every single day. This one point is so important for you to get. You will not become what God created you to be until you see yourself as He sees you.

Descriptives of you in God's eyes can only come from the Bible, not the labels of men/women. Man's opinion or words used by others to label you contrary to God's Word cannot and will not stand.

Words are like a mirror, whether God's mirror, the mirror of your life experience, or the mirror of the words of others. Whose mirror are you looking into? The one you are gazing into is the one that defines you today. If it's a mirror contrary to God's Word about you, put it down right now and start looking into God's mirror; His Word.

Let Go and Move Forward

In order to fulfill your purpose, you have got to let go of the past and surrender to the present, to move into the future. Sometimes people get stuck in their present because they are not letting go of an event of the past. Often, they don't even realize it. But, they know something is wrong; their dreams are dormant and their hopes are fading.

If this is you, you must accept your identity in Christ and your unique purpose, then put everything and everyone else under the microscope of those truths to make sure they support, encourage and inspire you to do more for Christ than you ever thought possible. If those things—people, personal thoughts, etc—come against your identity and purpose, remove yourself from them. Change your thinking; replace the thoughts that are contrary to God's Word with truths from the Scripture and keep doing it until your thoughts line up with what God says.

Regarding people, love people, but realize they are seasonal. Most are only in your life for a short season. Ask the Lord to help you sift through your relationships and reveal the people He has chosen for your journey, then kindly separate yourself from those who are not Divinely placed on your path.

Do not judge this based on whether you like or dislike someone, whether they are difficult or burdensome. People are placed in our life to produce growth in us. Sometimes people rub us the wrong way because God is creating a pearl in our life and theirs.

Either way, be sure that you are moving forward in your own spiritual growth as you endeavor to fulfill the purpose God handpicked you for.

Your purpose can only be fulfilled by you; you with the help of the Holy Spirit. Be willing to go it alone, just you and the Lord, then He will add to you the right people at the right time.

Since you are handpicked by Him, so too will those be that come along side. There's nothing more valuable to advancing the Kingdom of God, than a company of people handpicked for a powerful purpose and divinely placed and moving in unity together for God's glory.

Application & Activation

Settle this…

- You have an ultimate call; Christ-likeness.
- You are uniquely purposed by God.
- Faithfulness to God and His way brings increase.
- You have a God-given gift or talent; often more than one.
- There is a mirror image you are reflecting today.
- You have got to let go of the past and surrender to the present, to move into the future.

Scripture meditations …

John 15:16
"You didn't choose me. I chose you. I appointed you to go and

produce lasting fruit, so that the Father will give you whatever you ask for, using my name."

2 Corinthians 3:18

"So all of us who have had that veil removed can see and reflect the glory of the Lord. And the Lord—who is the Spirit—makes us more and more like him as we are changed into his glorious image."

Ephesians 2:10

"For we are God's masterpiece. He has created us anew in Christ Jesus, so we can do the good things he planned for us long ago."

Journal & pray ...

Write out two reflections. What do you see in the mirror today? What should the reflection be in light of how God sees you? Ask Holy Spirit to give you specific details about your unique identity and purpose. He will! Write it out.

Surrender to Freedom

"Tomorrow's freedom is found in today's surrender." – Unknown

Cease Resistance!

Self-denial is the essence of surrender and as you let go of your incessant need to be in control (I'll be first in line!) and invite the Spirit to lead you, God takes over and liberty is realized.

Liberty or freedom comes by not just knowing but practicing the fruit of the knowledge; God *IS* in control. He has laid the plan out, and He is in charge of bringing His plan to pass by opportunity.

Greater liberty comes when you surrender more and more to the Lord. I love that Carrie Underwood song, "Jesus Take the Wheel" a perfect analogy of surrender. It's like being in a self-driving car except, Jesus is driving. The thought of this is refreshing to me. It takes the pressure off, so that you can have a pure and full relationship with the Lord while He fulfills all of His purpose in your life.

Your part is only to daily inquire of Him as to His desires for you in the moment. To do what is necessary and possible, allowing Him to do the impossible.

Why is it so hard to surrender? The unknown is frightening. We can't control what we can't see. We can't anticipate, maneuver, get ahead of or stop if it gets out-of-control or goes beyond our comfort zone.

Even though it can be hard at times, we must prepare ourselves for an uncertain future where hopes and dreams come to pass by surrendering everything to the hand of an uncompromising, all-powerful Creator.

Large and In-Charge

This becomes easy as we remind ourselves that we are not in charge of fulfilling His promises, He is. And He is not just able to take care of all that concerns us but willing to get involved and do it. And, He desires to work on our behalf because it is His plan and purpose not ours. He is large and in-charge of it all.

> **"We are not being asked to surrender to one who will take us captive, but to the One who will captivate us with His love, acceptance and blessing."**

What has God asked you to surrender to Him? Let go of it quickly, because there is something amazing He wants to add to you to replace the things He asked you to lay down.

Derek Prince once said, "God will give back to you abundantly when you are willing to [surrender] to Him."

It's one thing to ask a soldier to surrender to an enemy, but quite another to ask a rebel to surrender to the one who has his best interests at heart. You see we are not being asked to surrender to one who will take us captive, but to the One who will captivate us with His love, acceptance, and blessing. The One who will catapult you into His Divine plan for your life. It's a win-win for God's people who will never be put to shame or be defeated by an enemy. No! He desires that we fly, that we obtain all He has promised us. Everything our Father gave to us through His blessing and His Son Jesus Christ.

My heart overflows at the thought and I wonder who in their right mind wouldn't want to surrender to such a Captivator? He is the captor of your heart and mind with the intent to hold you in His presence, to protect you from all impending danger and to deliver you from every adversary. His only desire is that you commune with Him in Heaven throughout all eternity. Not as servant, but friend and heir. He invites you to rule and reign with Him.

See that you do not resist Him, but surrender quickly to His loving hand. When you surrender, it will require a heart that responds to the promptings of the Lord.

He draws you closer by prompting you with His presence, love, joy, and peace. His promptings can feel like a blanket of warmth, a flood of love overflowing from your heart, a still small voice in the heart. When you hear, or recognize His presence, quickly respond by prayer, obedience, and worship. Let Him know you recognize He is near. I promise you He loves the sound of your voice when you call. Surrender will open a greater window for communication with your heavenly Father, so don't be surprised when you feel Him draw near[1].

Go Ahead, Jump!

I like to compare surrender to freefalling, like jumping out of an airplane without a parachute. Now mind you I would never literally do this, but I think of it often in comparison to surrendering everything and everyone, as I remind God my life is His to do with as He wills.

Don't be afraid to "freefall" with God. He answers when we call, He catches when we fall, and He reveals every step at the right time and in the right way. Don't resist these uncertain moments but take much joy in each one as part of the greatest adventure of your life. He has set you up for victory, given you all things that pertain to life and godliness[2]. You have all the powers of heaven backing you up.

Your Helper in this God journey, the Holy Spirit, leads, guides, and teaches you all things. As you follow His leading, you yield more and more to the Lord and the result is freedom. Paul declared this freedom to the Corinthians as He proclaimed, "Where the Spirit of the Lord is, there is liberty[3]!" The Greek word for freedom is "eleutheros," meaning; delivered, unbound, unshackled and set free[3].

As we yield our heart, mind and body to the Holy Spirit, His task is to transform us into the image of Christ. We are no longer conformed to the world but transformed by the renewing of our mind. The Scriptures reveal that our mind is renewed by exposure to, acceptance and application of the Word.

God's Word is our blueprint for living. Dive head-long into His Word, read it over and over again, and walk it out daily. As you do, you conform your heart and mind to Him, surrendering more and more to His purpose. The end result is unwavering faith in God.

In the process, you are being equipped for your call and set at liberty to realize your destiny in Christ.

Application & Activation

Settle this…

- When you surrender, you draw near to God and He draws near to you.
- Freedom & liberty in Christ come through surrender.
- God IS in control.
- You have a Helper on your God journey; the Holy Spirit.
- Every answer you need is in the Word of God.

Scripture meditation …

James 4:8a
"Come close to God, and God will come close to you."

2 Corinthians 3:17
"For the Lord is the Spirit, and wherever the Spirit of the Lord is, there is freedom."

Journal & pray …

Identify the areas of your life where you feel pressure or driven to control events and people. Write out how things would be different if everything was in order and peaceful. Ask Holy Spirit to help you release those matters to God so that He can work them out for your good. Repeat!

Why? Because this is an exercise in faith, not a miraculous moment. You will have to do this over and over again until you learn there is nothing God can't or won't do on your behalf. And, that when He does it, it will be better than anything you could imagine.

4

Fully Equipped

God doesn't call the qualified,
He qualifies the called. – Unknown

I don't know who first uttered the words above but they are as true as true can be. Here's an even longer discourse to reinforce my point;

> *Isaac was a day dreamer, Jacob was a cheater, Peter had a temper and denied Christ, David had an affair and tried to cover it up with murder, Noah got drunk. Esther was an orphan, Elijah was suicidal, Jonah ran from God, Paul was a murderer and he was way too religious.*

> *Timothy was young and inexperienced, Gideon was insecure, Miriam was a gossiper, Martha was a worrier, Thomas was a doubter, Sara was impatient, Elijah was moody, Rahab was a prostitute, Samson – he liked prostitutes. Isaiah preached naked for three years, John the Baptist ate bugs and had second thoughts about the very Messiah he baptized.*

> *Jeremiah was way too emotional, Moses stuttered, Zacchaeus was short, Abraham was old and Lazarus was dead. God doesn't call the qualified, He qualifies the called!*

> – Unknown

Can you locate yourself in there somewhere? I can, in fact, I can locate myself in more than one example. The truth is we are all unqualified. But we are wholly loved, approved, gifted and chosen by the Father for great works in His name.

If God chose only those who were already qualified by education, title, strength, etc., He would never get any glory for anything that is or was accomplished for the Kingdom of God on earth. Qualified people don't need to trust anyone other than themselves, their intelligence, title, education, etc. God resists the proud[1], but gives grace to those who acknowledge their desperate need for help.

Not Of Ourselves

You can see this idea of God choosing the "qualified" is not theoretically possible according to the New Covenant of Grace. It's by grace we are saved, not of ourselves, lest any man should or would boast[2]. It's the work of God's grace by the power of the Holy Spirit that qualifies us, each and every day that we choose to walk with the Lord.

This "qualifier" or hikanoó in the Greek according to Colossians 1:12, means to properly reach a state of sufficiency, abled, or competent[3]. We are made adequate by gradual growth, step-by-step as our faith increases.

Increase is accomplished by choosing God's ways as life unfolds and challenges present themselves. Each time we choose to have faith in the Lord and walk through the circumstance, God's presence increases upon our life[4]. Our capacity for Him is enlarged and the next time adversity comes, we are better prepared to meet it with faith than we were the previous time.

God chose us in Christ. He chose us before we were ever in our mother's womb. He chose us before we were saved by faith in Jesus Christ. And, He chooses to use us for His glory *from babes to full grown followers.*

The Most Unlikely Ones

He uses the simple things to confound the wise. Like a fisherman to be the "rock" upon which He would build His Church. Like a Religious Zealot who imprisoned and murdered Christians, to write more than half the New Testament.

God always chooses the most unlikely ones, the weak ones, the exact opposite of those who the world would choose. Like the shepherd boy David who rose up in the name of the Lord to slay lions and bears, a giant, and multitudes of God's enemies to become Israel's King. His own family didn't think him worthy enough to even call him from the sheepfold to be considered by the Prophet Samuel[5]. But God!

> **"God always chooses the most unlikely ones, the weak ones, the exact opposite of those who the world would choose."**

Not one of Christ's disciples were of the Synagogue. Only one was of noble descent; Bartholomew. All were wandering sheep of sorts. One of my favorite lines between Jesus, Peter and Andrew, "Follow Me and I will make you fishers of men[6]." Changing perspectives from working sweat and brow daily for food and money, to working with love as an instrument in the Father's hand to draw men to Christ. Talk about a paradigm shift.

Not one of them were "qualified" to be apostles, prophets, evangelists, pastors, or teachers. They worked with their hands and mind, not their heart. But God in His infinite wisdom purposed and positioned each of them to do exactly what they were doing when Christ came calling. And each profession they were in had prepared them to become exactly who God designed them to be.

God used them and will us right where we are too. Then through life experience, teaches and trains us up in the ministry to maximize our gifts and talents for the benefit of others.

The Qualifier

The only qualification is if you be Christ's, a believer, if you pick up your cross and follow Him daily, and if you endure with patience throughout your life.

There's no limit to where God will take you. When you prove yourself faithful with what He has given you, He will give you more and more and more and more. You, my friend, have been created for MORE!

There's no limit to how deep or high He will take you in knowledge, understanding and wisdom. The more you seek Him the more you find. You grow in knowledge of Him through the Word. Be a student of the Scripture, search out matters and learn how the Lord would respond to each situation, then follow His lead. As you do, you will learn and grow and become all the Father created you to be.

God has given us help to in the form of His leaders; the five-fold ministry of apostles, prophets, evangelists, pastors and teachers. Each one called to equip you for the work of the ministry. Their mission is to help you come to full stature in Christ, a believer who is able to speak the truth in love[7].

If you are Christ's, you are called and fully qualified for the task at hand. You are to be a demonstration of Jesus to the world and in the process, share the gospel, and do the work of the ministry. As you do, all will see you are different, unique, and inspirational. They will follow you, because they see you are following Jesus Christ.

Application & Activation

Settle this…

- God chooses to work with the unqualified.
- God gives strength to the weak.
- God uses the simple to confound the wise.
- There is no limit to where God will take the faithful.
- The only "qualifier" is if you be Christ's.

Scripture meditations …

James 4:6
> "And he gives grace generously. As the Scriptures say, "God opposes the proud but gives grace to the humble."

Ephesians 2:8 & 9

"God saved you by his grace when you believed. And you can't take credit for this; it is a gift from God. 9 Salvation is not a reward for the good things we have done, so none of us can boast about it."

Matthew 4:19
"Jesus called out to them, "Come, follow me, and I will show you how to fish for people!"

Journal & pray …

Have you ever disobeyed the Lord because you felt unqualified to do what you felt in your heart He was asking you to do? If so, choose someone in the Bible mentioned in the quote on page 23, read the account of what that person did for God and note all the shortcomings in his/her life. Write in your journal all the things God did with that person in spite of his/her inadequacies. Now, ask Holy Spirit to help you obey God's promptings in detail the next time He asks you to do something with full faith that it is Him working in and through you for others.

5

Arrayed in Splendor

For He has clothed me with garments of
salvation, He has wrapped me with a
robe of righteousness... Isaiah 61:10

You are a beautiful, handsome, amazing creation. One-of-a-kind, unique, not another like you. And, there's a group of people, in your field who are appointed to be fruit on your tree. God gave them to you, yes you, not to anyone else. He gave them to you, to steward each one for His glory.

You are a people magnet, honey in a bottle, attracting every person around you. The good, the bad, the ugly, the broken, the abused, the wounded, the angry, the somber, the depressed, the oppressed, the burned out, burned up, thrown out, and stomped on. All of them, they come to you for Christ.

It's that atmosphere around you, the light in your eyes, peace on your face, swelling of love emanating from you, that God uses by His Spirit to draw hearts to Himself.

> **"You are a people magnet, honey in a bottle, attracting every person around you. All of them, they come to you for Christ."**

You are God's exhibit! On full display for all the world around you to see! So own it! Own the understanding of what your splendor is purposed to do in the lives of people. It is not for you, but them. You enjoy the benefit of His presence, but He rests on you for others.

Your Lord is King of Kings! He has decked you out in palace style. The Psalmist declares in 45:13, "You are glorious within; your clothing wrought with gold. Your value exceeds ten trillion, of trillions. No one has the ability to assess your worth; it is far above all of man's calculations and estimates."

This is what the Word and your heavenly Father have to say about you. When will you believe it? When will you actually release the beautiful flow, He has placed deep in your spirit? It's time to own it! Own your identity. Own your atmosphere.

It's Time to Get Dressed

When Paul exhorted believers to "put on" the new man[1] which is in Christ Jesus, he was telling us to wear Him like clothing. In fact, a word study reveals that phrase literally means to *sink into a garment*. What a thought! I will sink into Christ, heavily lean into Him, wrap Him around me and live.

When we wear Christ like clothing, we are *arrayed* in the splendor of His presence and power. "Put on" also means to be *endued* with a special quality or ability. He is your royal adornment and elegant beauty. The result is you walk in the light, in the power of Holy Spirit, in complete "sonship" as an heir of God's promises, and through love come into the bond of perfection.

The test of wearing Christ is the ripening of spiritual fruit[2] in our life; love, joy, peace, longsuffering, kindness, goodness, faithfulness, gentleness, and self-control. When demonstrated, these spiritual character traits confirm we are fully clothed in Christ.

Can you imagine the power released in our words and actions as we *intentionally* speak and do what Christ spoke and did? Life-changing, family-changing, neighbor-changing, city-changing, state and nation-changing, world-changing! It's up to you to *intentionally* put Christ on and let Him live through you.

The Perfect Partner

There are many references in Scripture that reveal you are in Christ. You are in Him and He is in you! The perfect partner, the One who leads, the One who instructs, the One who bestowed the best upon you in the form of Himself. What a thought! Makes my spirit leap at the thought of it! Of Him!

> **"When you put Christ on, He should be the first thing people recognize about you."**

Author Max Lucado once penned a powerful thought. I'll rephrase it here for the men who will read this book; *the hearts of those who follow Christ should be so hidden in God that those looking for them have to find Christ first[3].*

When you put Christ on, He should be the first thing people recognize about you. There's something different, something so right, kind, peaceful, generous, and loving. In Him you stand out from the crowd and everyone looking for answers will come straight to you.

We often don't believe there is anything special, valuable, or significant about us. We don't realize that construction is taking place on the inside erecting an edifice over you. This "construction" is taking place in the spirit-man, the very heart of who we are as God created us to be. And He will bring to completion this work He has begun for all the world to see[4].

You are God's Building

It is the very heart of man that will be displayed to the world. This is accomplished by living from the inside out. Those who live from the outside in are tossed by every wind, subject to the world's ways not submitted to God's.

But those who intentionally live from the inside out (Led by the Spirit, walking in the Spirit, doing what the Scripture teaches us to do.), will never be moved or shaken.

I know, you are one, who will take your stand with God. Stay steady and keep moving forward with Him. Because of your commitment and dedication to Him, you will be like a tree of life to all who wander into the vast shade your tree provides.

This outward display is a manifestation of the inward condition of the heart that overflows with the very nature of our God. The presence of God flowing from you draws many to the field where you are planted, growing, and thriving.

You will stand firm in the day of shaking since the unshakeable Kingdom has been established in your heart. You must believe this and receive it now. Settle it in your heart and train your mind to stay focused on Jesus, His Word, and the mighty name of our God.

You are sealed up in Christ, with the guarantee of the Holy Spirit. But are there chinks in your armor? Openings where falsity can creep in whether by thoughts or attacks. Doubt is your biggest foe, doubt fuels fear, and fear will paralyze you.

Power will flow from your life as you live and walk in Him. All the doubt, fear, and worry will fade away, because you have squarely put your faith and hope in Him. You are wearing Christ and the presence of God proves it!

Application & Activation

Settle this…

- You are created to display God's glory & presence.
- You are adorned and endued with His power.
- You must put on Christ like clothing, saying and doing what He says and does.
- You change the atmosphere because of God's presence that lives inside of you; live from the inside out.
- Own your identity and atmosphere.

Scripture meditation …

Psalm 45:10—15
"Listen to me, O royal daughter; take to heart what I say.

Forget your people and your family far away. For your royal husband delights in your beauty; honor him, for he is your lord. The princess of Tyre will shower you with gifts. The wealthy will beg your favor. The bride, a princess, looks glorious in her golden gown. In her beautiful robes, she is led to the king, accompanied by her bridesmaids. What a joyful and enthusiastic procession as they enter the king's palace!"

Ephesians 4:24
"Put on your new nature, created to be like God—truly righteous and holy."

Journal & prayer …

Write down ways that you can change the atmosphere around you in conversation, prayer, and daily living. Ask Holy Spirit to remind you when you are in a situation that you can bring heavenly change to with your words and actions, then do what He shows you to do.

6

A Presence of Power

"One man with God is a majority."
– Brother Andrew, God's Smuggler

Brother Andrew, Andrew van der Bijl, is a missionary from the Netherlands who smuggled Bibles into Communist nations during the height of the Cold War years.

Son of a blacksmith, Brother Andrew didn't even finish high school. But God used this ordinary Dutch man, with his bad back, limited education, without sponsorship and no funds to do things that many said were impossible. From Yugoslavia to North Korea, Brother Andrew penetrated countries hostile to the gospel to bring bibles and encouragement to believers[1].

God uses ordinary people like Brother Andrew *and you* to do extraordinary things for His glory. It's not just the occasional plan of God to do such things, but a common happening for any person who is willing to be used by God. Brother Andrew did exactly what God put in his heart even though many cautioned him and suggested his plans would never succeed. With God though, nothing is impossible for those who believe. Brother Andrew knows it and firmly believes "One man with God *is* a majority."

Degrees, Pedigrees, & Man's Approval

Problems arise when we think we have to have a degree and a title before God will use us and man will approve and accept us. We disqualify ourselves in this presumption and deny God's power and ability. Ultimately, we make the power of God in our lives of no effect and never fulfill the best of God's plan.

We allow the fear of man to take root in our heart and we become man-pleasers rather than God lovers. Man-pleasers always seek the approval of men. They go the way of the crowd, never taking the narrow path that leads to life. When the least little bit of disapproval comes whether perceived or actual, man-pleasers quickly realign with men to stay in their good graces.

This is dangerous, it's a snare that brings deception and destruction, bringing us to another character trait that hinders the presence of God's power in believers; self-consciousness.

Self-conscious or God-conscious?

Often man-pleasers have a lack of confidence. The World teaches people to have self-confidence. Society spends a lot of time and money developing self-confidence, but self-confidence is not what believers need. Christ's followers need to put their confidence in God, not in their own strength or the strength of men. Believers need to have immovable and unshakeable faith in Him, not in themselves.

Do you retreat, when you know God has said, "Go!" Do you disappear into the crowd when God told you to "Lead?" Do you fall silent, when you know God said, "Speak?" If you are not doing what you know God has created you to do, then you are shrinking back into obscurity because of self-consciousness.

Now is the time to allow Holy Spirit to remove every man-pleasing root from your heart. Now is the time to renew your faith in God and remind your "self" it's not about you, it's about Him. The things He has ask you to do He has already given you the victory for. You will succeed and sometimes your success won't involve another person. It will be you and God alone!

God's Presence & Approval is All You Need

The One True God, the Creator of the Universe, the God Who speaks ALL life into existence, the God of peace, the God who heals, the God who is a banner over your life, resides inside of you. The God who said "Light be!" and light continues to increase and give birth to universes far above and beyond this earth realm. He LIVES in you!

Think of that for a moment. Get a revelation of this, ALL of the powers of heaven are in YOU! And you are in Him! Paul summed it up perfectly, "in Him you live, and move and have your being[2]." You are *one* with Him and He is one with you. In fact, Jesus' last prayer was a request to the Father that we would be one together with Them, just as They are one[3].

So then, since you are living in Him and Him in you, there is a presence of God's power with you all the time. He is with you wherever you go, always available to you.

Things get sticky when people don't realize their place in God and simply don't ask God to get involved in their life. We have not, because we ask not or ask amiss[4].

The key to releasing His power is *acknowledgement, relinquishment,* and *rest!*

Acknowledgement

Acknowledge the power that lives on the inside of you. ALL of the power of heaven resides there. The power that was released when Jesus died on the Cross and the power that resurrected Him from the dead. The power that parted the Red Sea, the power that created light, firmament, man and woman. The power that raised Lazarus from the dead, opened blind eyes, deaf ears, tied tongues, and vexed minds. The power that healed the sick and sent demons scrambling to embody the swine. It's all in YOU! You!—Yes YOU!

God's power is not going to be released until you acknowledge it and release it in every situation. And, it's not that hard to release God's power either! You do it in prayer by asking in Jesus' name. You release God's power by asking Him to get involved in situations and circumstance in your life and the lives of those around you. You release God's power by declaring His Word and having faith in Him and His promises.

Ephesians 3:20 gives us a BIG CLUE about how *acknowledgement* works in releasing the power of God. "Now to Him who is able to do infinitely more than all we ask or imagine, according to His power that is at work within us…"

According to HIS POWER! When we ask about a matter God needs to get involved in, by His power He is able to do and has already done more than we can even think. This is a great example of the fact that God has numbered our days. He formed and fashioned them before we were in our mother's womb. He knows what we have need of before we ask[5]... But He still waits for us to ask before He gets involved. Why? This reinforces in us a need for Him and a sense of humility in acknowledging we can't do anything or be anything without Him.

We are growing from faith to faith with each need. We ask, He answers, He provides. The waiting time between asking and receiving is where growth takes place. We are growing in faith and therefore going from glory to glory or ever increasing presence and power in our life.

This presence of power is growing with each challenge and it's also growing as we, like John the Baptist, decrease so that Christ can increase in our life[6]. The more of Christ you have working in and through your life, the more power is being released through you.

Relinquishment

What must you do? *Relinquish* all personal power, control, sin, etc. Trust me! The Holy Spirit will reveal every matter to you so that you can let go!

> **"God will not release His power until you relinquish yours."**

God will not release His power until you relinquish yours. It can be tricky when you first relinquish. We have been created to accomplish or to do, to live. Often the very strengths we've been given for God's glory are weaknesses until we realize there's nothing we can do in our *own strength*.

When we relinquish our power, we give our gift to God for His purpose and at that moment God's strength and power are released.

Rest, yes rest

Then, rest! *Rest!* Why did I say rest is a part of releasing God's power? Because rest is a part of God's plan, not just for man, but creation too.

Let's look at nature first. We see rest in farming. The land must rest for a period of time. Why? Because it produces a greater crop after the rest. Minerals are restored, moisture, etc. The soil becomes fertile again.

My friend your life is no different. You need rest and when you rest, richness, beauty, peace and order result.

Restlessness in the Lord is a very harsh place to live. When we do not rest, we are weary, lack focus, and become irritable. We live in a place where God cannot get through.

When we value rest like God values rest, then we see an increase of His power flowing through our lives. Rest will also bless your family and every place around you where you interact with people. You will be spiritually sharp, walk in wisdom, and have an answer.

From this place of rest, you will be able to reflect, recharge, and refill. It's a time when God Himself will download new things into your spirit that are filled with strategies you need for the days ahead.

This presence of power that is already upon your life is working in you for the benefit of others. The whole of humanity is desperate for the sons of God to be fully endued with power. When this happens, the entire world will be turned upside down just like it was in the days of Acts.

At that moment, you will be fully arrayed, walking in God's power and fierce for Christ!

Application & Activation

Settle this...

- There is a presence of God's power flowing from you.
- All you need is God's approval; not man's.
- Be God conscious!
- Acknowledgement, relinquishment and rest will release God's power in your life.

Scripture meditation ...

Acts 17:28
"For in him we live and move and exist. As some of your own prophets have said, 'We are his offspring.'"

Matthew 6:8
"... your Father knows exactly what you need even before you ask him!"

Journal & prayer ...

Write out what relinquishment and rest looks like for you today. What do you need to relinquish to the Lord? How can you honor God in your rest? Ask Holy Spirit to show you what true rest in God looks like.

7

Fierce in Battle

"...the people who know their God will
be strong and do exploits." – Daniel 11:32b

Wouldn't you like to have a friend who steps into the middle of every battle in your life? Sure, you would! Who wouldn't? Problem is most people you know don't have the capacity to stand and fight with you when the moment requires their help.

Here's the deal with God, He fights every single battle in your life. You need only position yourself, stand still and watch Him work.

You see, the fight is fixed in your favor. All the Lord asks us to do, is stand, endure, believe, obey, speak, wait, watch, and pray.

> *"Through You we will push back our adversaries; Through Your name we will trample down those who rise up against us. For I will not trust in my bow, nor will my sword save me. But You have saved us from our adversaries; And You have put to shame those who hate us. In God we have boasted all day long, and we will give thanks to Your name forever."*
>
> ~ Psalm 44:5-8

Fierce Warrior Sheep

I want to share a dream with you that I had in 2004. The dream sequence begins on a cliff in New Zealand. My husband, Chuck, and I were enjoying the terrain watching a herd of sheep grazing the dewy grass. I noticed how fluffy and content the herd was as they went along together.

Out of nowhere a pack of wolves attacked them. Terror rose in my heart, but suddenly the sheep turned on the wolves and utterly destroyed them. I remember shuttering at the carnage, thinking those beautiful little sheep were as fierce as a lion. I woke up, heart pounding and wrote this dream down in my journal and never forgot it.

This was no ordinary dream. It was prophetic, a foretelling of the future. I asked God about those killer sheep. And, what I needed to take away from the dream in revelation. I know now it is for today.

God's people are the flock of Jesus Christ, His sheep. He is the Great Shepherd; leading and guiding them in the way they should go. They are sealed with the guarantee of the Holy Spirit; the Spirit of Truth who leads them to victory.

Jesus also gave them His name, His Word and His shed Blood which are the power that secures their victory. By putting His Spirit in them, His Word is living and dynamic and deep within the heart of each one.

We Will Push Back & Trample Down

In this hour, God's people, who know Him, will not stand by in silence when attacked by Hell's minions. No! They will rise up in His Name, in His power and authority. They will push back and trample down the adversary with the spiritual weapons God gave them.

These fierce saints are covered from head to toe with His armor, equipped to take down every enemy that comes against the Kingdom of God. Ephesians 6 describes this battle and the armor; helmet of salvation, breastplate of righteousness, loins girded with truth, feet shod with the preparation of the gospel of peace, shield of faith, and sword of the Spirit[1].

They are fierce in battle and they understand the battle too. They know they are not at war with people but with principalities and powers and rulers of darkness[2]. It's a spiritual battle. And, they will overcome by the blood of the lamb and the testimonies they declare, all the while not loving their own lives[3]. They are God's fiercest sheep. They stand against all the tactics of the enemy and they will not move until there is victory.

You are called to stand among these fierce warrior sheep; to worship, to pray; and to proclaim His Word. What are you doing in each of these functions? You should be declaring God's glory, majesty, and honor. You're not talking about yourself, your circumstance, or matters of this world. You are talking about Heaven's power over everything!

Let God arise and His enemies be scattered!

Be strong and Take Action

You may not recognize your strength, but that only means you are in Him. God always chooses the most unlikely ones. Among His deliverers are children, women, prostitutes, orphans, adulterers, and murderers. He uses the simple ones to confound the wise.

Put on your armor, pick up your sword, and take your stand in Him. Many will run and hide behind you as they recognize God is with you. In your presence, they will see Him and desire what God has given you for the benefit of all of humanity.

Sometimes all you need to do is SHOW UP!

When God's people come on the scene everything changes. The presence of God on their life turns darkness to light, death to life, and sorrow to joy! How? They own their atmosphere. They have a revelation that wherever they are, heaven comes to earth.

> **"Put on your armor, pick up your sword, and take your stand in Him."**

As Daniel 11:32b says, "The people who *know* their God will be strong and do exploits." This word "strength" in the Hebrew (chazaq) has a rich meaning. Those who *know* God will prevail, be courageous, resolute, and fierce[3].

These are the people who know God, not just know of Him, but know Him by intimate knowledge through relationship. Here are just a few synonyms of what it means to "know" in the Hebrew language; acknowledge, disciplined, endowed, taught, and skilled[4].

These are not casual believers. They are all in, sold out, completely surrendered, fully committed followers of Jesus Christ. They are not moved by what they see either, they know the voice of the Shepherd, and refuse to follow a stranger. They will display strength and take action when the times demand it.

Take your place among the mighty. Position yourself, stand firm, and witness the victory of the Lord.

Application & Activation

Settle this…

- God fights every single battle in your life; you win!
- You are among God's fierce warrior sheep.
- You have to put on your armor.
- The battle is fought in prayer; not hand to hand with people.
- Sometimes your presence full of God is enough.
- When you know your God, you will be strong.

Scripture meditations …

Ephesians 6:13—17

"Therefore, put on every piece of God's armor so you will be able to resist the enemy in the time of evil. Then after the battle you will still be standing firm. Stand your ground, putting on the belt of truth and the body armor of God's righteousness. For shoes, put on the peace that comes from the Good News so that you will be fully prepared. In addition to all of these, hold up the shield of faith to stop the fiery arrows of the devil. Put on salvation as your helmet, and take the sword of the Spirit, which is the word of God."

Ephesians 6:12

> For we are not fighting against flesh-and-blood enemies, but against evil rulers and authorities of the unseen world, against mighty powers in this dark world, and against evil spirits in the heavenly places.

Journal & prayer ...

Write out the areas of your life where a battle is unfolding in the Spirit. Make a daily plan to visualize yourself putting on your armor and taking a stand in faith. Ask Holy Spirit to get involved and help bring the victory.

8

You Have the Answer

"Silver or gold I do not have, but what I have I give you: In the name of Jesus Christ of Nazareth, get up and walk!", —Peter to the Lame Man

This lame man did not need what he thought he needed. He needed to be able to walk so that he could live the abundant life Jesus died to give him.

Think of it, this man lay there every day at the Beautiful Gate asking for money, completely stripped of all dignity. He had no choice in the matter either. He was living the cards life dealt him. But, God had a different plan!

Not only did God have a plan for this man, but a plan for every person who witnessed his miraculous restoration.

What I Have, I Give

Do you realize this is God's plan for you and everyone who crosses your path? It's His plan for every situation and circumstance you find yourself in. To bring Christ into a lost and dying world by whatever means is necessary. You need only pray and ask God to give you keen insight and awareness of everyone in your pathway. You need discernment and answers with God's wisdom to share in the moments when God is prompting you to speak.

Oswald Chambers once said, "The dearest friend on earth is a mere shadow compared to Jesus Christ." He is right. I'll take it another step. The dearest friend on earth would never let another person finish their life without Christs.

Peter did not have what the lame man wanted, he had what the lame man needed. Every person on the face of this earth needs what Peter gave him. You too should be eager to give to everyone what they need most; Jesus. In addition, to salvation, people need peace, joy, love, forgiveness, etc. They need! Are you willing to give?

Never Miss an Opportunity

Missed opportunities will be the saddest reminder that we didn't share Christ when an open door presented itself to us.

Paul exhorted Corinthian believers to preach the Gospel to everyone. He was free, yet made himself a slave to all to win as many as he could to Christ. Without violating God's Word, he said he became all things to all men that by all possible means he could win some[1].

You too can be all things to all men, without compromising, so that you may win some. This simply means you meet people where they are in life. If you want to bring salvation to people, you have to go to the unbeliever. If you want to bring healing to people, you have to go to the spiritually and physically sick. If you want to bring hope to people, you have to go to where hopeless people dwell.

You have to learn how to maneuver your interactions with people who do not believe, either at all or the way you do. You have to be willing to engage them in conversation that is life-giving so that you can influence them for Christ.

Daniel and his friends maneuvered King Nebuchadnezzar's Court by proclaiming God in the midst of life and death situations. The end result of their trials, Father showed Himself mighty and many wanted to know the God Daniel and his friends served.

Daniel served in the courts of many foreign kings. He would also rise to Magi, a recognized wise man, who was not required to take on the system of believing in many gods, but continue in the belief of the One True God of the Universe. He was the only Magi whose God was Jehovah and those who followed Daniel made his God their God, Jehovah.

Even Ruth knew that Naomi's people and her God were the people and God she would cling to. She recognized the difference and the power and provision of the Faithful One who healed and restored His people. Unlike the false gods of Moab, she found the life and peace of those who served El Elyon, God Most High.

> **"You have access to all the answers needed by every person on your path."**

You Have the Answer

Daniel and Ruth both had the answer when called upon. And for that matter so did Joseph, Deborah, Esther, and Elijah just to name a few. God's people who seek Him and serve Him will always have an answer for every situation. Whether in the king's court like Daniel, the family like Ruth, or in the church, marketplace, community or government, God's people always have the ability to bring God's wisdom.

You too have the answer every person on earth is dying to hear. You have access to all the answers needed by every person on your path. The veil of separation has been removed. The Throne Room is open to you 24/7. We can go boldly before Him in our time of need to get exactly what is necessary for every situation[2]. He said, "Call to Me and I will answer you, and show you great and mighty things you did not know[3]."

The One answer you have that *EVERYBODY* needs is Jesus! How often do you share Christ with people? I find that most people are too timid to share the Gospel. They lack the courage or confidence to talk with others about the Good News.

Why would anyone withhold good news? Especially when we live in a world with a 24-hour-news-cycle that reports bad news over and over again. Bad news creates fear in the heart, trepidation, and apprehension. Good news makes the heart leap for joy, giving a sense of hope and relief. People want good news, you ought to be quick to give it.

You have access to the Throne of Grace, the presence of God and to the ministry of the Holy Spirit who reveals all things to you that He hears the Father say and the things that are to come.

When you find yourself in circumstances that are not godly or where a person or group needs an answer, just like King Nebuchadnezzar needed in Daniel's day, you will pray and ask for answers and you will receive wisdom from heaven, so accurate that those who hear will be astonished and amazed.

You are the one, you have power and authority to obtain the answer and to declare it to whoever needs knowledge of it.

You Have Positional Authority

Positional authority refers to your position in the Kingdom of God and the authority God has given you in the earth. It is significant friend. Let me summarize your positional authority.

First, God gave us authority and told us to subdue the earth in Genesis 1:28. "Subdue" meaning in the Hebrew bring it into bondage. The earth and all God created is subject to you. Of course, you were created for good, to produce life and fruit. He also gave you dominion over the earth; meaning to "rule."

Second, Jesus gave us authority over all the power of the enemy; "authority" in the Greek meaning power, moral authority, influence and conferred spiritual power.

Problem is we don't understand our authority, nor exercise it. Today, settle it in your heart that you have been given power from on High, in the name of Jesus to destroy the works of the enemy, a power and authority that is conferred to us through Jesus.

You have authority, you are not subject to the world, Satan, or unbelievers; all are subject to you. You have the power of the name of Jesus, the Blood of the Lamb and the Word of God. You have wisdom, insight, keen awareness, discernment regarding every matter. You need only ask. If you believe you lack wisdom, James said ask for wisdom from God and He will give it to you in abundance.

You are Divinely Placed for a Powerful Purpose

It is no mistake at all that you find yourself where you are today. With God, there are no coincidences. He chose you for this moment and He also formed the words in your spirit that you will speak. You need only step forward and deliver the answer God put in your heart.

I can hear even now some of the thoughts of those who will read this book. What if I'm wrong? What if I lose friends? What if I get in trouble?

I understand that it is not always easy to say what God is telling you to say. Trust me though, once you release His words there will be a confirmation from those who hear. They will tell you that the words you spoke are the answer they were waiting to hear.

The hardest part is jumping your fear. Once you do though, you will be an unstoppable force for the Gospel. And, the more you put fear under your feet by acting on what you believe God is showing or telling you to do, the less and less you will feel the enemy trying to stop you.

Case in point, when I was first called to minister in the prison it seemed every day I was scheduled to go in, all kinds of things went wrong. Issues with my home, my family, my dog, my car, my job! Here's the good news though, the more I stepped over those issues and served God, the less the issues manifested, confirming it was a spiritual matter.

As I'm writing this, I keep hearing that old secular song by M. C. Hammer, "Can't Touch This." Can you hear the beat? I digress...

As soon as the devil realizes he is not going to shut you down, intimidate you, or get you to forfeit God's plan, he will stop touching everything around you to stop you. Say this with me, "He can't touch this!" You, your family, your home, anything that concerns you. Now he might raise his ugly head now and again, but keep reminding him where he is... under your feet. Go ahead and do a tap dance on his head, he can't stop you or God's plan, even when you mess up.

Application & Activation

Settle this...

- You are Christ's, God's child, a son of God, full of power and light.
- You are sent by Him to bring salvation, healing, deliverance, and restoration to the world through Jesus.
- You are a partaker of the nature of God, full of His wisdom.
- You have the answers this world desperately needs.
- You are willing to deliver the news; Good News!

Scripture meditations …

1 Corinthians 9:19—23

"Even though I am a free man with no master, I have become a slave to all people to bring many to Christ. When I was with the Jews, I lived like a Jew to bring the Jews to Christ. When I was with those who follow the Jewish law, I too lived under that law. Even though I am not subject to the law, I did this so I could bring to Christ those who are under the law. When I am with the Gentiles who do not follow the Jewish law, I too live apart from that law so I can bring them to Christ. But I do not ignore the law of God; I obey the law of Christ.

When I am with those who are weak, I share their weakness, for I want to bring the weak to Christ. Yes, I try to find common ground with everyone, doing everything I can to save some. I do everything to spread the Good News and share in its blessings."

Journal & prayer ...

After meditating on Paul's words above, write out the names of people who represent some or all of the groups mentioned. Write out a plan to meet them where they are and bring Christ to them. Ask Holy Spirit to set up interactions and give you His Word and timing for each plan.

9

Now, Let's GO!

*"There is only one way to avoid criticism:
Do nothing, say nothing, and be nothing."* –Aristotle

*"The question isn't who is going to let me; it's
who is going to stop me."* -Ayn Rand

This chapter is worthy of two important quotes. Why? Because putting feet to your faith is often where people fall short.

The Weak & The Least

It can be hard to get going! Ask Gideon. He was so concerned he really heard God that he set several fleeces to confirm and still had to whittle down every move he made to completely obey God and fulfill his purpose. Nonetheless, as Gideon kept obeying God's instruction, the victory was assured, and all he and his army had to do was show up, blow their trumpets, break their pitchers, carry torches and declare the words, "The Sword of the LORD and of Gideon[1]."

Gideon's faith was stretched to the max with every move and in the end, there would be no denying God Himself had given the victory. How? 300 men vs. innumerable men. Not a sword in their hand at first confrontation. The enemy turned on each other and ran just because

Gideon's army blew their trumpets and broke their pitchers. I know, I know... it makes no sense to the natural mind, but God is not natural He is SUPER-natural, always confounding the wise and strong with the simple and weak. Sound familiar?

I remember myself, the words of Holy Spirit when I kept asking, "Are you sure God? Me? Really? Me?" As clear as a bell I heard, "Consider My servant Gideon."

Why did Holy Spirit whisper that in my heart? Because Gideon reminded God he was the weakest and the least[2]. Yeah right! I'm not surprised. God always chooses the least among us to show His mighty works to the world. Now there's a self-portrait for the masses.

I'd say, if you didn't tremble with fear or question at the thought of going in the name of the Lord, there's something yet to be perfected in you. We should all tremble at the thought of representing Jesus, speaking for Father, and hearing Holy Spirit.

We only get our legs under us as we realize we are doing what we were created to do and that we are getting it right the majority of the time. Most people never start because they are afraid of failing or being persecuted for their belief. But, this one resistance leaves them feeling unfulfilled and discontent. The last place God created them to live.

Give Him Your "Yes!"

There's a joy that comes as we say "Yes Lord," a fullness of heart that cannot be compared to anything. True contentment only comes when we know that we know that we know, we are doing exactly what God called us to do.

Say "Yes" even when you don't fully understand what God is asking you to do. Your "Yes!" signals your surrender. Much like Jesus in the Garden of Gethsemane; "Not My will but Yours be done" (Luke 22:42).

Jesus knew exactly what he was surrendering to, but think of Isaiah in this same vein.

Isaiah was vexed in his heart because of the perversity of his people and his own lips, which he said were "unclean." At that moment, an angel came with hot coals touching them to his lips to purify him.

Then Isaiah heard a question from Heaven, "Who can I send, who will go for us?" He immediately answered and said those famous words, *send me*[3]. At that moment, Isaiah had absolutely no idea where he was going. Talk about surrender, this is a pure leap of faith. Evidence that Isaiah had already determined in his heart he was going to go with God not matter what it would cost him. After all he had experienced visions of the future and recognized the corruption of his countrymen and nation, well before this vision. However, the call was not made clear until the moment Isaiah said "Yes!"

> **"Say 'Yes' even when you don't fully understand what God is asking you to do."**

The purification of his lips prepared him to speak as a Prophet for God.

Jesus too was prepared for the events that would unfold after his arrest in the Garden. *After* He said, "not My will but Your's..." *Then,* an angel came and strengthened Him[4]. Heaven made Him ready for every confrontation that lay before Him; not before the surrender, but after.

Please make note of this in your heart. Many are waiting for God to do something, while God is waiting for their surrender. Their "Yes!" God wants your "Yes!" Give Him your "Yes!" today and every day.

I Had a Thought God Had a Plan

This is a phrase I coined years ago, and I believe it is the absolute truth. I had a thought, God had a plan. God's plans were not what I thought, but they were greater than anything I could imagine. If I can think it, God has already gone above and beyond my thoughts (Ephesians 3:20).

Recently I heard Joanna Gaines of Fixer Upper fame say something that struck my heart. On a "White Chair" interview for I Am Second, she said, "If I didn't have Chip Gaines in my life, I'd still be dreaming in my head not acting on any of it or living it out." Then she turns to him and says, "You pushed me, you pushed me out of my comfort zone[5]."

Are you living your dreams in your imagination or are you living your dreams as you actually walk them out? Because, the plans of God for your life—your dreams—are greater than anything you can imagine. Start living His dream for your life, start today.

As you consider your dreams, know this, God is the One who gave you a passion, desire, and talent. He is the Author of your dreams that include a desire to be all He created you to be and do everything He created you to do.

There are no coincidences with Him. You are His and He is orchestrating every move, every opportunity, every person. For example, When I first felt a desire to do something for the Lord, I wanted to right the wrongs I had committed through my own decisions. My heart's desire drew me to a ministry that helped individuals at a moment when they were making the same decision. This was a time of healing for me and a time for me to experience the blessing of ministry; we always receive way more than we give.

From this season of service, I found my place in the local church, first children's ministry, then music, then women's Bible study, prayer ministry, mission work, teaching and leading small groups, prison ministry, homeless ministry, and on and on. Now I'm a pastor, influential voice, author, worldwide speaker, and still a little God girl.

Faithfulness ALWAYS Leads to MORE

Why do I share this with you? To demonstrate how our faithfulness always takes us to a greater place of service to the Lord. It is true that when you prove yourself faithful in that which is least, God will make you ruler over much.

"Launch out into the unknown, because that's where power is released and miracles happen."

Jesus spoke these words in the Parable of the Talents giving us an example of three servants who received talents from their master. The servants did not receive the same talents, each was given talents *according to his/her ability.* The first servant received five talents and doubled the five. The third got one talent and did nothing with it because of fear[6].

I guarantee you the faithful servant who doubled the five talents also began serving the master with one talent. He proved himself faithful and continued to increase in talents. This is true of you and me, when we are faithful with one, we get two; with two, three, with three, four and so on.

We must resist the human tendency to fear the unknown and be faithful with the talent God has given to us. If it's music sing or play, if it's encouragement; encourage. If it's communication; speak. Do not be shy, be bold and courageous, fervent and joy-filled.

Often people wait on something to happen, but God is asking you to have faith in Him and leave the comfort zone Joanna Gaines spoke about. It takes courage to leave what is familiar and launch out into the unknown, but that's where power is released and miracles happen. You don't want to miss out on the best of what God has planned for you!

And, you cannot fail! Receive what I am saying to you today, "YOU cannot fail." You will have setbacks, challenges, questions, and moments of wanting to give up, but if you refuse to quit you will succeed. Period. End of story.

Now what? Well, it's time to put feet to faith!

Go and Tell

Back to Isaiah for a moment. After he boldly declares "Send me," then God said "Go and tell!"

The Hebrew meaning of these two words is powerful and significant. Let's look at "go" first. "Halak" means to access, become greater, brighter, grow steadily, flow, follow, involve, lead, live, and spread. You can see some of your purpose is wrapped up in this word "go."

Then "tell," in the Hebrew "amar" means to address, advise, answer, declare, demonstrate, designate, resolve, and speak. Again, a further understanding of what God was saying to Isaiah, "Go and tell this people…"

As you go, you will access God's power, become greater, shine brighter, grow in Him steadily and continually. You will flow with Holy

Spirit as you follow Him; leading, living, and spreading the Good News of Jesus Christ to every person you encounter along the way.

This is God's plan for you and purpose as you… Go tell. And it's not a far-off time to come. It is right now, it is your time. In the immortal words of Mordecai to Queen Esther… "And who knows but that you have come to your royal position for such a time as this?" And… you have! So, let's take the next step.

The Who, The What, The How

We've already established the Who, YOU, and the What, the gospel of Jesus Christ. Your unique purpose in sharing the gospel with your gifts and talents for the glory of God.

Now the How. The How comes with open doors and opportunities. When you say "yes" to God, He establishes intersections in life with the people and places where your gift and talent will flourish for Him.

It may be at church and it may not be. Like me you could end up ministering at a homeless shelter or a prison. Don't stress about it today, just ask the Lord to open a doorway of opportunity for you to use your gift for His glory.

As you do the future will unfold in a most glorious way. And, you will be trusted with more as you grow in grace, faith, and glory!

Application & Activation

Settle this…

- God uses the least among us.
- Say "yes," then you will be empowered for His purpose.
- Go and tell whoever God sends you to.
- Your faithfulness will always lead you to more.
- God will open a doorway of opportunity.

Scripture meditation …

Luke 22:42—43
"'Even so, not what I want, but what You want.' An angel from heaven came and gave Him strength."

Matthew 25:21
"'You have done well. You are a good and faithful servant. You have been faithful over a few things. I will put many things in your care. Come and share my joy.'"

Journal & prayer …

Write out what you believe your God-given purpose is today. Who are the people God has asked you to influence with the Good News of Jesus Christ? Ask Holy Spirit to open doors of opportunity and lead you to the place where these people are located.

10

Epilogue: The Future of YOU

*"It is not only going to be the rain, the former rain
and the latter rain, but [God] is going to give
to his people in these last days a double portion
of His power."* – Tommy Hicks

Tommy Hicks was a key-leader in the Argentinean Revival of 1954. To say he was a fervent minister of the Gospel, Evangelist, and Revivalist would be an understatement. He witnessed God do amazing miracles throughout his life in ministry.

In July 1961, by his own account, his perception of the Body of Christ, the Church, in the last days would change dramatically. God gave him a vision of the Body three times in exact detail revealing what His Church would look like and do throughout the earth.

I first learned about this vision around 1999. It stirred my heart so much, I've held onto God's plans revealed through it, watched for it and expected every detail to come to pass. If it didn't line up with Scripture I would have dismissed it immediately, but I believe its veracity is confirmed by the Word.

You can read the entire vision and Tommy Hicks' commentary on my website and I encourage you to read it. Watch and expect with me. There is a day coming when the earth will be filled with the glory of God, He will pour out His Spirit on all flesh, signs and wonders will abound (Not for you and me, but the unbeliever.), the Word of God will run unhindered throughout the entire earth, and a mighty harvest will be reaped with great joy as a result.

Hicks shares that the great theme in the lives of those end-time believers is Jesus Christ and a flow of Divine love; here's an excerpt:

> *"These men and women are of all walks of life, degrees will mean nothing. I saw these workers as they were going over the face of the earth. When one would stumble and fall, another would come and pick him up. There were no "big I" and "little you," but every mountain was brought low and every valley was exalted, and they seemed to have one thing in common – there was a divine love, a divine love that seemed to flow forth from these people as they worked together, and as they lived together. It was the most glorious sight that I have ever known. Jesus Christ was the theme of their life. They continued and it seemed the days went by as I stood and beheld this sight. I could only cry, and sometimes I laughed. It was so wonderful as these people went throughout the face of the whole earth, bringing forth in this last end time."*

This vision was a confirmation for me of a picture God gave me in a time of prayer in 1998. I was standing in the middle of raging flood waters, but was not overtaken. Everything around me, everyone, was overcome by the waters. I asked the Lord why I was able to stand in the middle of the current without even a wobble. He said, "This is not a flood as you know a flood to be. It is a flood of My LOVE and in the days ahead it will overtake everything and everyone in its path."

Imagine that, God's love pouring out like a flood throughout the earth. Talk about a world-changing moment!

I believe with all my heart the Tommy Hicks' vision came from God and it will come to pass in the days ahead. I also believe, YOU and me, we have been chosen for this time to participate with God in His plan and purpose for all men. I believe that "God's love" will set us apart, because Jesus said so. The whole world will know we are His by our love for one another[1].

YOU are not here by accident my friend, there's nothing random about you, not one thing. You are Divinely placed with a powerful purpose! You are a key-player in God's end-time move. And this is what I see ahead!

The Future of YOU

It all began thousands of years ago, when you were thought of and planned by the greatest Planner of all time and eternity.

In that moment, you were handpicked by God for His purpose; blessing, goodness, and glory.

You didn't realize it initially, but once you met Christ and surrendered your life to Him, you found freedom and liberty as you grew in your knowledge of truth.

Step by step, day by day, month by month, year by year, Holy Spirit equipped you and gave you revelation of your God given talent and opportunities to share the Good News of Jesus with family and friends.

The more you've come to know who you are in Him, you realize and accept the unique beauty given to you by the Father.

His captivating love beckoned you come closer, allowing Holy Spirit to make you more and more Christ-like, you recognize God's presence and power.

His Word and promises become a reality in your life, you step into your authority in Him and become fierce in battle. There's not a challenge you don't overcome, an adversary you cannot defeat, a room you do not fill with the beauty of His holiness flowing from you.

While others ask questions, seek and search for wisdom, you step in to speak. All eyes turn, every mind asks the question, "Who is this person." They recognize God is with you, they come, they ask, they seek, they inquire, they want to know, they have to have the peace in you, the grace you dispense, the love that flows so easily, the graciousness and thankfulness you extend in every circumstance.

They are hungry, they are thirsty, they are empty. But YOU ARE FILLED and READY. You've been chosen by God, equipped by heaven, clothed with light, life, and Christ. You are the embodiment and demonstration of all that is good and blessed in Him.

The whole of creation has been waiting for your appearance. Isaiah saw a vision of YOU, he proclaimed the coming Messiah Jesus Christ and the latter-day events. He spoke of the glory of God filling the earth and resting on His people. Even in gross darkness, unbelievers will recognize you and come to the light of His glory that shines so brightly through you[2].

You are amazing. You are powerful. You are not just living out your days, you are making history everyday as you live your Divine purpose in Christ.

YOU are not here by accident!

Application & Activation

Print this…

The above Future of You is a "word painting" that suggests the future God has for you from this moment forward. Print it out at the following link and keep it in your Bible or somewhere you can read and refer to it often. Ask Holy Spirit to establish every part of this beautiful epilogue of YOU in the days ahead.

Link: www.charlanakelly.org/The-Future-of-You

Notes

Introduction:

    1. Isaiah 40:28 – 31, emphasis on verse 31.

Chapter 1: God's Story of YOU

    1. John 15:16

    2. The Passion Translation, for more information visit: http://www.thepassiontranslation.com/

    3. Colossians 1:13

    4. Learn more about John Calvin, 1509—1564 at https://calvin.edu/about/history/john-calvin.html

Chapter 2: Handpicked for Purpose

    1. Definition of "Handpick;" online Oxford English Dictionary, published by Oxford University Press https://en.oxforddictionaries.com/definition/hand-pick

    2. Jesus & Paul said believers are chosen; Jesus in John 15:16; Paul in Ephesians 1:4

    3. Greek word for "chosen" (eklegó) **HELP™ Word-studies** copyright © 1987, 2011 by Helps Ministries, Inc.

For complete text and additional resources visit: HelpsBible.com

    4. 1 Timothy 2:4 and 2 Peter 3:9

    5. Romans 4:20

    6. James 1:17

    7. Ephesians 2:10 (NLT)

Chapter 3: Surrender to Freedom

    1. James 4:8a: draw near to Him and He will draw near to you.

2. 2 Peter 1:3

3. 2 Corinthians 3:17, Freedom; Greek word for "Freedom" 1658 eleútheros (an adjective) – properly, free (liberated), unbound (unshackled); (figuratively) free to realize one's destiny in Christ. **HELP™ Word-studies** copyright © 1987, 2011 by Helps Ministries, Inc.

For complete text and additional resources visit: HelpsBible.com

Chapter 4: Fully Equipped

1. James 4:6

2. Ephesians 2:8 & 9

3. Qualifier – "hikanoó" in the Greek according to Colossians 1:12; **HELP™ Word-studies** copyright © 1987, 2011 by Helps Ministries, Inc.

For complete text and additional resources visit: HelpsBible.com

4. 2 Corinthians 3:16-18

5. Samuel Anoints David 1 Samuel 16

6. Matthew 4:19: I will make you fishers of men.

7. Ephesians 4:11—16

Chapter 5: Arrayed in Splendor

1. Ephesians 4:24

2. Galatians 5:22

3. Original quote by Max Lucado: "A woman's heart should be so hidden in God that a man has to seek Him just to find her."

4. Philippians 1:6

Chapter 6: A Presence of Power

1. Inspirational Christians, Brother Andrew Biography: http://

www.inspirationalchristians.org/brother-andrew/

2. Acts 17:28

3. John 17, The Jesus Prayer

4. James 4:2c—3

5. Matthew 6:8, Jesus, leading up to The Lord's Prayer

6. John 3:30

Chapter 7: Fierce in Battle

1. Ephesians 6:13—17 The Armor of God

2. Ephesians 6:12 The Spiritual Battle

3. Revelations 12:11

4. **HELP™ Word-studies** copyright © 1987, 2011 by Helps Ministries, Inc.

For complete text and additional resources visit: HelpsBible.com

Chapter 8: You Have the Answer

1. 1 Corinthians 19—22

2. Hebrews 4:16

3. Jeremiah 33:3

Chapter 9: Now, Let's Go!

1. Judges 7:20

2. Judges 6:15

3. Isaiah 6:8

4. Luke 22:43

5. I am Second White Chair Interview: Chip & Joanna Gaines http://www.iamsecond.com/seconds/chip-and-joanna-gaines/

6. Matthew 25:14—30

Chapter 10: Epilogue: The Future of YOU

1. John 13:35

2. Romans 8:22 Creation groans; Isaiah 60:1—5 God's glory fills the earth

About the Author

Charlana Kelly, a dynamic speaker and teacher, delivers her message through multiple mediums laced with a clear passion for winning souls, making disciples, and raising up leaders to win nations for Christ.

She has been in full-time ministry for more than 20 years, serving in various ministerial capacities in churches, nonprofits, and as a part of community service programs. She is the author of the books, "Reaching Out with a Message of Hope" and "In Search of the King's Court." She also developed and wrote the discipleship program, "Tools for Triumphant Living" which has been used in ministries, transitional homes, jail and prison reentry programs.

Charlana has preached the Gospel and empowered leaders around the world through missions since 1998, drawing multiple thousands from four nations while in Kitale Kenya. She continues to reach out around the world through her podcast, A Voice for Our Time (Listen/Subscribe on iTunes) and LIVE Front Porch Talks (Connect with her on Facebook). In 2015, she founded SpeakTruth Media Group, LLC which produces and publishes all of her ministry media works.

She became a licensed minister in 2000, then ordained in 2002 by Dr. Jim Kaseman of the Association of Faith Churches & Ministers Intl. She is currently an associate pastor with The Fellowship at Larry Bruce Gardens with Pastor Larry Bruce in Kennard, Texas. She is actively involved in her community through the Houston County Ministerial Association and contributes to community-wide prayer and events. Charlana also serves on the Board of the Patriotic Remnant, a California-based media ministry with a focus on prayer for our nation.

While her ministry accomplishments are far reaching, Charlana believes firmly that her highest calling is at home. She and her husband of 30 years, Charles, reside in Crockett Texas. While they never had children of their own, God has given them many spiritual kids over the decades. Witnessing those "kids" grow in Christ has brought them much joy!

For more information, visit charlanakelly.org where she provides resources to connect, learn and grow in Christ.

Invitations & Contact Info

Charlana is currently open for invitations to speak at your church/ event and would love to hear from you. She resides in East Texas; however, she will travel within the US and to other nations. She has spoken at churches and conferences both large and small in the US as well as Haiti, India, Kenya, and Jamaica.

Please contact by email, charlana@charlanakelly.org, to initiate an invitation for ministry at your church, conference, event or workshop. Please include some details, so we can get the scope of the vision you have for your event.

Charlana prayerfully considers the times and seasons of the Lord and His plans for His people throughout the earth. She is always honored and blessed to be a part of ministry to and for the Body of Christ. Over the years, she has often been the primary speaker at events, however she loves being part of a team of speakers and enjoys watching God use the dynamics of different ministers to bring salvation, healing and restoration to His people.

Mail: PO Box 1448, Crockett TX 75835-7448

Email: charlana@charlanakelly.org

Connect, Learn, & Grow

Social Media

Facebook – Charlana Kelly

Twitter – Charlana Kelly

YouTube – Charlana Kelly

Other Books by Charlana Kelly

In Search of the King's Court © 2006

Reaching Out with a Message of Hope – Seven Vital Keys to Outreach Ministry © 2007

Weekly e-Devotional

DayBreak, sign-up at website: charlanakelly.org

Podcast – iTunes
A Voice for Our Time

LIVE Front Porch Talks on Facebook